BUILDING BLOCKS OF GEOGRAPHY

OCEANS

Written by Izzi Howell

Illustrated by Steve Evans

WORLD BOOK

a Scott Fetzer company
Chicago

World Book, Inc.
180 North LaSalle Street
Suite 900
Chicago, Illinois 60601
USA

For information about other World Book publications,
visit our website at **www.worldbook.com**
or call **1-800-WORLDBK (967-5325).**
For information about sales to schools and libraries,
call 1-800-975-3250 (United States),
or 1-800-837-5365 (Canada).

Library of Congress Cataloging-in-Publication Data
for this volume has been applied for.

Building Blocks of Geography
ISBN: 978-0-7166-4275-6 (set, hc.)

Oceans
ISBN: 978-0-7166-4284-8 (hc.)

Also available as:
ISBN: 978-0-7166-4294-7 (e-book)

WORLD BOOK STAFF
Executive Committee
President: Geoff Broderick
Vice President, Editorial: Tom Evans
Vice President, Finance: Donald D. Keller
Vice President, Marketing: Jean Lin
Vice President, International: Eddy Kisman
Vice President, Technology: Jason Dole
Director, Human Resources: Bev Ecker

Editorial
Manager, New Content: Jeff De La Rosa
Associate Manager, New Product:
    Nicholas Kilzer
Sr. Editor: Shawn Brennan
Proofreader: Nathalie Strassheim

Graphics and Design
Sr. Visual Communications Designer:
    Melanie Bender
Sr. Web Designer/Digital Media Developer:
    Matt Carrington
Coordinator, Design Development:
    Brenda Tropinski

Acknowledgments:
Writer: Izzi Howell
Illustrator: Steve Evans
Series advisor: Marjorie Frank

Developed with World Book by
White-Thomson Publishing LTD
www.wtpub.co.uk

Additional spot art by Samuel Hiti and
Shutterstock

TABLE OF CONTENTS

There is a glossary on page 40. Terms defined in the glossary are in type **that looks like this** on their first appearance.

WHAT IS AN OCEAN?

My salty water isn't so good to drink. Yuck!
But that doesn't mean that the oceans aren't useful or important.

I'm home to many different animals and plants.

People depend on lots of ocean animals for food.

The ocean stops our planet from getting too hot or too cold by absorbing heat from the sun.

Without the ocean, we wouldn't have certain medicines. Scientists study how ocean sponges and corals are able to fight infectious bacteria and use their findings to develop new medicines.

There wouldn't be any pearl jewelry either. Pearls grow inside oysters and some other shellfish.

There's a little bit of the ocean on your dining table - the salt in the salt shaker!

Gas and oil are found deep beneath the ocean floor. These resources can be burned to provide energy.

The movement of the **tides** can also produce energy. Tidal energy is renewable and doesn't create any pollution!

It's even possible to remove salt from seawater, so that the water can be used for drinking and industry.

OCEAN 1
The oceans are also an important transport link. Ships carry products and people around the world.

Land ahoy! Oceans are so great that it's no surprise that 80 percent of people live within 60 miles (96.5 kilometers) of an ocean **coast**!

MAJOR OCEANS AND SEAS

The Arctic Ocean is the smallest ocean. The North Pole is near the middle of the ocean.
The shores of the Mediterranean Sea are popular with tourists.
The Indian Ocean is the warmest ocean, on average.
SEA OF JAPAN
Many ships catch fish in the Sea of Japan.
ARABIAN SEA
MEDITERRANEAN SEA
SOUTH CHINA SEA
Violent storms called typhoons often whip up the warm waters of the South China Sea.
The Arabian Sea is an important trade route for ships.
INDIAN OCEAN
The Southern Ocean surrounds Antarctica.
The region where the land meets the ocean is called the *shore*.

Let's wave hello to my good friend Land!
Nice to "sea" you!

When I meet up with Land, we make some pretty exciting coastal features! Let's take a look!

Let's start with an easy one - a beach! This is an area of sand (my favorite!) or pebbles along the coast.

Powerful ocean **waves erode** (wear away) rock along the shore, creating steep cliffs.

Helllooooooo?
Waves can also cut caves and natural arches into the shoreline.

Waves pick up **sediment** (tiny pieces of sand and rock) and drop it farther along the coast. This can create new sandy features.
A spit is a **ridge** that sticks out into the water.
A bar traps water, creating a new lagoon.
A tombolo connects an island to the shore.
A lagoon is an area of seawater that has become partially or totally separated from the sea. The water in a lagoon is shallow.

A bay is an area of the coast where the sea is surrounded by land on three sides.
The land that sticks out on either side is called a headland.

USA
MEXICO
GULF OF MEXICO
A very LARGE bay is known as a gulf. The Gulf of Mexico is bordered by the United States and Mexico coastlines.

Some bays are very small! They are known as coves or inlets.

A reef is just an underwater ridge that lies close to shore. It can be made of coral or rock, or even created by humans!
If I say reef, I bet you think coral, right? But there's much more to reefs than that!

Tiny animals called corals create coral reefs. These animals live and grow together in colonies, forming beautiful limestone structures.
A coral reef is home to many ocean animals and plants.

People make artificial reefs for several reasons. Reefs protect the coastline from storms...

...and are good places to farm shellfish, such as oysters!

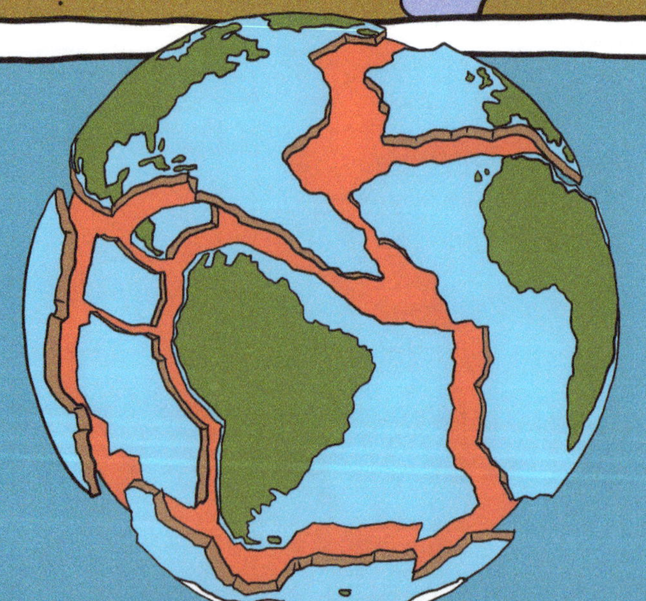

The outer surface of Earth is called the **crust**. Earth's crust is split into huge sections, called **tectonic plates**, which move very slowly.

Tectonic plates are made out of two types of crust – continental crust and oceanic crust.

Even though I'm in the ocean now, the ground beneath my feet is the same rock as that on land. It's all part of the continental crust.
Off the coast, the land goes down gently ...

... followed by a steep slope! Wooo!

Now I'm standing on oceanic crust. The ocean floor here is just like the land on Earth, with tall mountains, deep valleys, and flat **plains.** It's just hard to see it!

These mountains, the Mid-Atlantic Ridge, are mostly underwater. They form part of the longest mountain range on Earth. They are found in the center of the Atlantic Ocean, where two tectonic plates are moving away from each other.

Ridges like this form because heat from deep within Earth warms up the crust and makes it lighter and more flexible. This means that the ocean floor can rise to make a mountain!

If the plates move further apart, the crust will crack. Hot molten (liquified) rock comes up from under the ground.

The hot rock is cooled down by seawater and becomes a new section of the ocean floor.

When two plates move toward each other, one is pushed underneath the other. This can create a deep ocean **trench** (narrow valley).

The deepest known spot on Earth, Challenger Deep, is found in the Mariana Trench in the Pacific Ocean.

Challenger Deep is located 36,070 feet (10,994 meters) beneath the surface!

We don't know much about life in deep ocean trenches, as they are one of the least explored areas on Earth.

Only three people have visited Challenger Deep, but 12 people have walked on the moon!

The ocean looks and feels very different at different depths.

The deeper the water, the colder and darker it is.

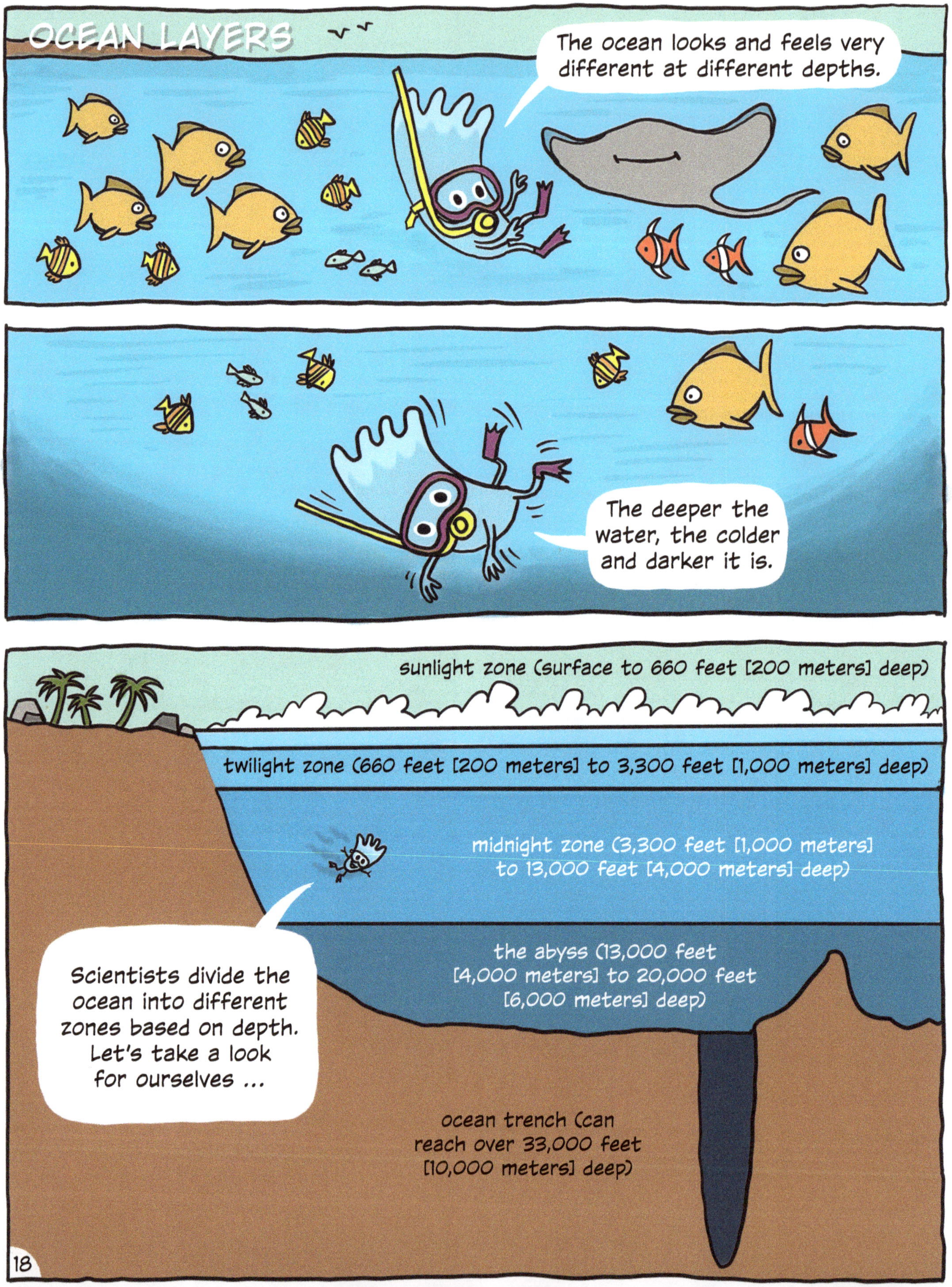

sunlight zone (surface to 660 feet [200 meters] deep)
twilight zone (660 feet [200 meters] to 3,300 feet [1,000 meters] deep)
midnight zone (3,300 feet [1,000 meters] to 13,000 feet [4,000 meters] deep)
the abyss (13,000 feet [4,000 meters] to 20,000 feet [6,000 meters] deep)
Scientists divide the ocean into different zones based on depth. Let's take a look for ourselves ...
ocean trench (can reach over 33,000 feet [10,000 meters] deep)

The top zone is known as the sunlight zone. As you might have guessed from the name, there is quite a lot of light here!

The sunlight zone is generally the warmest layer of the ocean, but it depends where you are!
Near to the equator, it can reach a tropical 86 °F (30 °C)

... but it's pretty chilly around the poles, dropping down to around 28 °F (-2 °C).

Most ocean plants and animals live in the sunlight zone.

Ohh, it's pretty dark now. We must be in the twilight zone. Almost no light reaches this layer of the ocean. This means that no plants can survive beyond this point, as they need sunlight to make their own food.

Now we're in the midnight zone.
The pressure is 100 to 1,000 times greater than the pressure on the surface due to the weight of all the water above!
And the temperature of the water is only just above freezing.

Eeek! An anglerfish. There are many animals in the deep ocean that are bioluminescent (make their own light), just like the anglerfish. It's one way that animals have adapted to life in these extreme conditions.

Some bioluminescent animals shine their light to attract prey, while others use it to scare off predators!

We're nearly at the sea floor now! The abyss is the final layer of the ocean in most places.
This layer is a bit like the dump of the ocean, as dead animals and plants fall down to the sea floor! It sounds gross, but it's an important source of food for the deep-sea animals that live down here.

But wait, there's more!
In some parts of the deep ocean near the boundaries of tectonic plates, water flows up from the ocean floor.

Oooh, that's nice and warm! The hot water coming out of this crack in the sea floor is called a hydrothermal vent. Hot rocks beneath Earth's surface have heated the water to 660 to 840 °F (350 to 450 °C)!

Such animals as mussels and giant tubeworms live around hydrothermal vents. But other than that, there isn't much life this far down.
I think that's a sign that I should head back to the surface!

OCEAN CURRENTS

The direction of the wind and the position of the continents make these currents move in huge circles called gyres.

If you're above the equator, a gyre moves clockwise ...
...and if you're below the equator, a gyre moves counter-clockwise!
This is known as the Coriolis effect. It can also be observed in storms.
The Coriolis effect happens because of the way Earth spins faster at the equator than at the poles.

Are you ready for an even bigger current? This one will take us all around the world!

It all begins here, in the Arctic Ocean.
When seawater gets very cold, it freezes.
The salt from the frozen water is left behind, making the surrounding water much saltier.

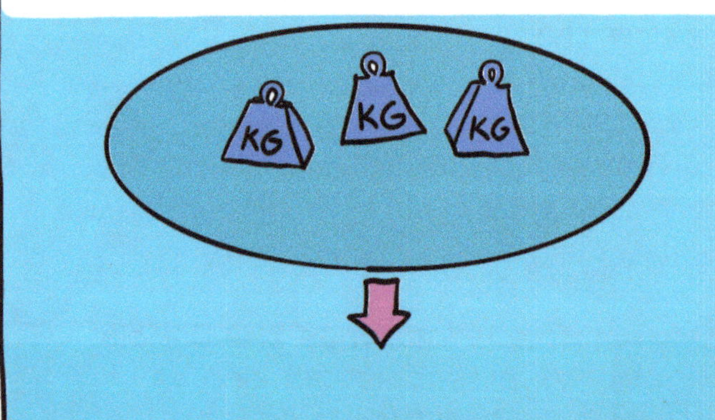

The extra salt makes this water heavier. It begins to sink toward the sea floor.
KG
KG
KG

The sinking water is replaced with water from the surface. This creates a current.
KG
KG
KG
Finally, more space for us!

ARCTIC OCEAN
PACIFIC OCEAN
ATLANTIC OCEAN
INDIAN OCEAN
SOUTHERN OCEAN
The deep water flows southward in the Atlantic Ocean to Antarctica.

Here, the ocean current is recharged for the rest of its journey! It gets colder and sinks again, keeping the current moving. These currents caused by changes in water density (heaviness) are deep-ocean currents.

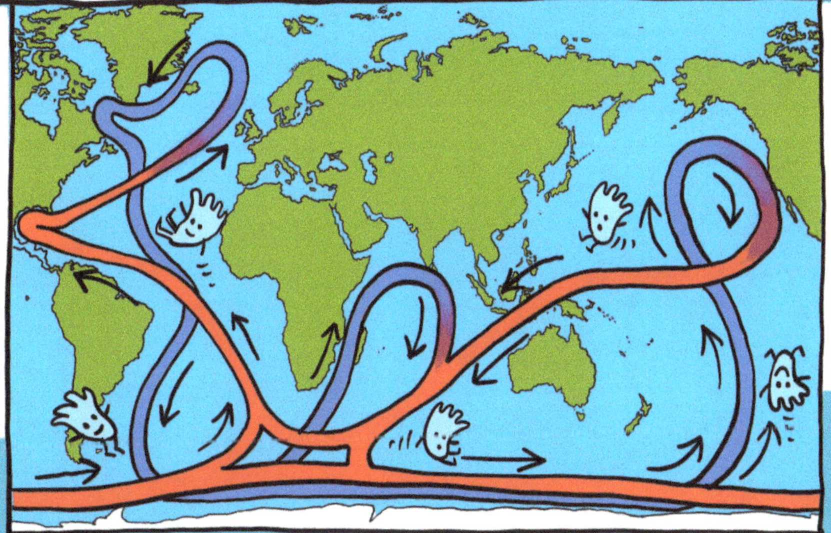

The current travels along Antarctica and then splits in two, with one half going into the Indian Ocean and the other to the Pacific Ocean.

The currents warm as they circle back around and return to the North Atlantic Ocean, where the cycle starts again.

It takes about 1,000 years for the water to complete this massive loop. What a journey!

This giant cycle helps to spread nutrients throughout the ocean.

Tiny **plankton** need these **nutrients** to grow and develop...

...and many ocean animals depend on plankton for food ...

...so currents are very important!

WAVES
Yo dudes! I love catching waves on my surfboard! But where do these waves come from?

People often think that waves are water moving across the surface of the ocean. But that's not right.

Waves are actually energy traveling through the water!
Hey, I'm Energy!

Water does move a bit in a wave, but it's an up-and-down movement instead of a horizontal movement.

Take this seagull, for example. When it is hit by a wave, it moves forward and up.

As the wave moves on, it falls back down to its original spot.

The water in the ocean moves in exactly the same way. We just can't see it!

So where does all this energy come from?
Did someone say my name?

Most waves are caused by the wind blowing on the water.

Big storms can drive huge waves to shore in a *storm surge*.

Tides are also examples of waves.

Earthquakes, landslides, and volcanic eruptions can set off massive waves called tsunamis.

Tsunamis can travel incredibly fast. In deep water, they can travel as fast as a jet airplane!

It's hard to spot a tsunami in the open ocean. As a tsunami gets close to shore, it suddenly increases in height.

If a tsunami hits land, it will destroy almost everything in its path. Luckily, there are several methods of predicting tsunamis, which provide enough warning time for people to evacuate.

TIDES
My castle! Where did all this water come from? It wasn't there when I started building.
Oh wait, I know what's happening here. Hello, high tide!
Every day, the sea level rises and falls along most coasts. This is known as the tide.
Hey, watch out for my feet!
At high tide, water covers more of the land.
At low tide, the sea level falls and more land is revealed. Time to get building again!
30

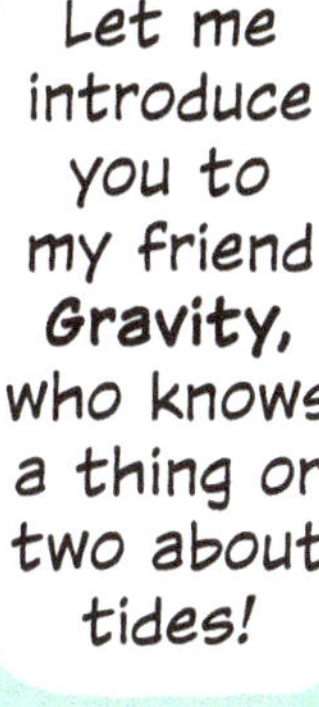

Let me introduce you to my friend Gravity, who knows a thing or two about tides!
Just thought I'd drop by for a bit!

Tides are caused by gravity from the moon and sun pulling on the oceans.
The area facing the moon and the area opposite the moon have high tides.
The other parts of the world experience low tide.

As the world spins, different areas of the planet experience high and low tides.

Crabs, mussels, barnacles, and seaweed live in tide pools. These pools are filled with seawater at high tide and left uncovered at low tide.

Tides can be dangerous.
In some places, the tide comes in quickly and can leave you trapped with nowhere to go. Always check the tide times and keep an eye on the ocean.

THE WATER CYCLE

The sun's heat makes water **evaporate** from the ocean, leaving salt behind.
My turn now! I'm now in a gas form called water vapor. Up I go into the air!

Brrr, it's chilly up here in the sky! The cold air makes water vapor change from a gas to tiny drops of liquid water. These droplets form clouds.

When a cloud can't hold any more water, it releases some of its load as rain or snow, which falls back to the ground.
The water drains into rivers, which flow into the sea...
...bringing the water back home to me!

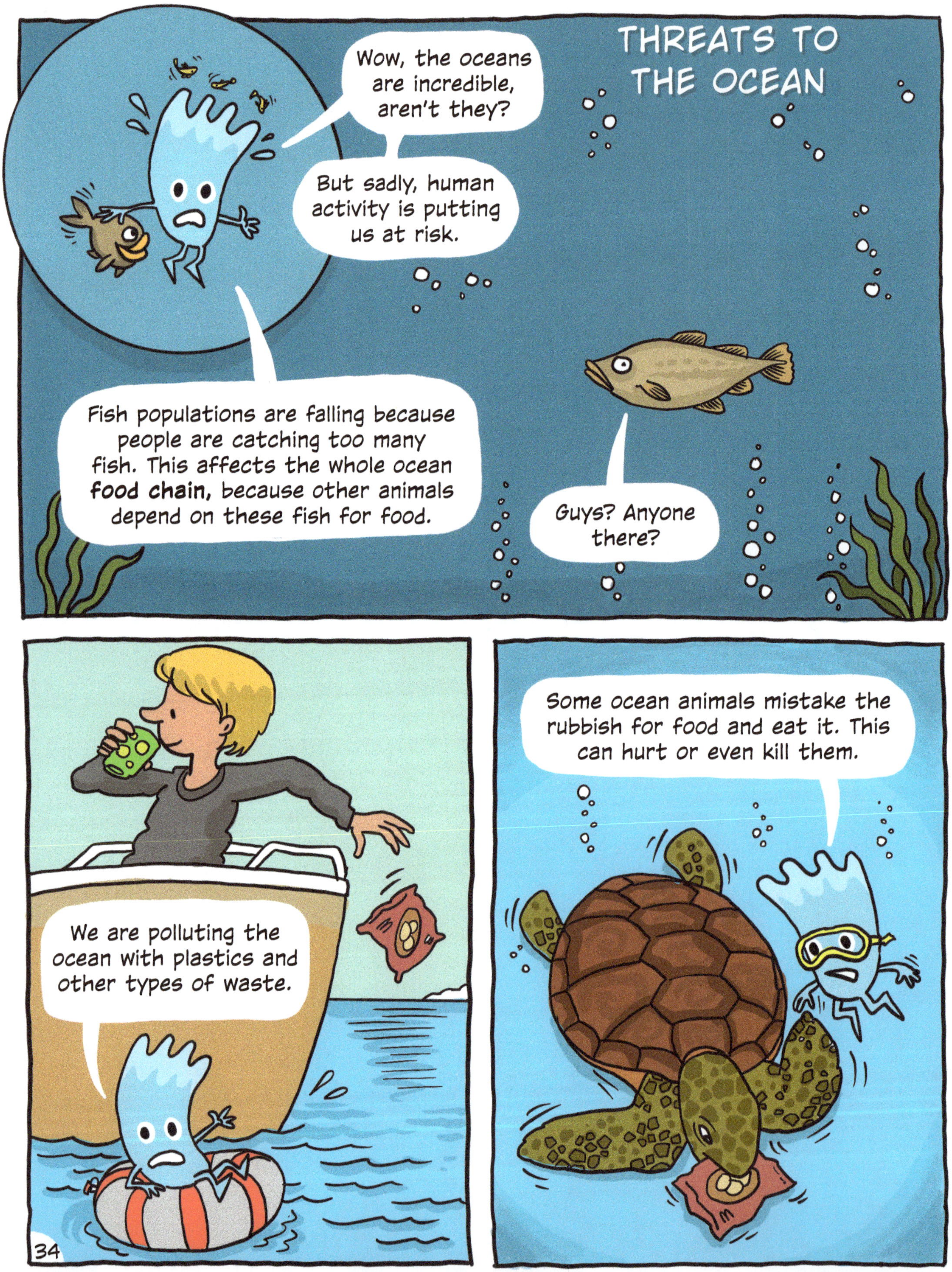

Wow, the oceans are incredible, aren't they?
But sadly, human activity is putting us at risk.
Fish populations are falling because people are catching too many fish. This affects the whole ocean **food chain**, because other animals depend on these fish for food.
Guys? Anyone there?
We are polluting the ocean with plastics and other types of waste.

Some ocean animals mistake the rubbish for food and eat it. This can hurt or even kill them.

Global warming causes the temperature to rise in oceans across the globe. Not all ocean life can survive in warm water.

Higher temperatures on Earth lead to ice melting at the poles.

The extra water added to the oceans is making sea levels rise around the world.
Many coastal areas are at risk of flooding.

It's not too late to save our seas! Governments, businesses—and even YOU—can help by using less plastic, burning fewer fossil fuels, and eating fish that aren't at risk.
Thanks for protecting the ocean and all of us in it!
STOP OCEAN POLLUTION
REDUCE GLOBAL WARMING
HANDS OFF OUR CORAL R
STOP OVERFISHING

QUIZ:
ROSCO'S WORLD CRUISE!

Rosco, the world-traveling rodent, is fascinated to learn about the many travel destinations that are in and around Earth's oceans and seas.

Each destination that Rosco wants to visit is found within or next to an ocean, a sea, or a smaller body of ocean water.

Take the quiz by applying the geography information you know. Use a good-quality world map or a globe to help you locate and compare places. You may also want to search the internet.

Here are the places Rosco wants to visit.
For each one, write the ocean, sea, or other
body of water where that location is found.

1. The white cliffs of Dover
2. Hong Kong
3. Cape Cod
4. Bass Strait
5. Ellesmere Island
6. Sri Lanka
7. Easter Island
8. Antipodes Islands
9. Malta
10. Nunivak Island
11. Cayman Islands
12. Andaman and Nicobar Islands
13. Azores
14. Cape Cormorin
15. Belcher Islands

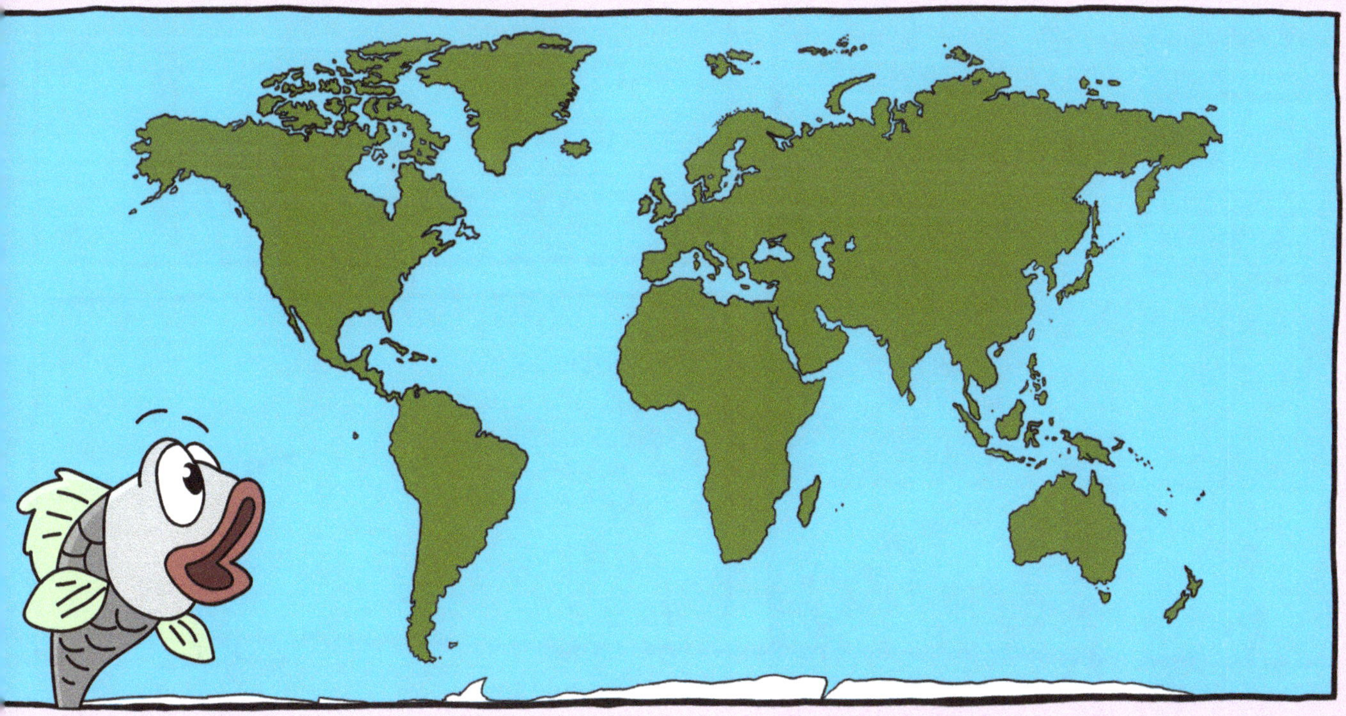

See page 40 for answers.

CAN YOU BELIEVE IT?!

A *tsunami* is a powerful wave usually caused by an earthquake or underwater landslide. A tsunami can reach speeds of 600 miles (970 kilometers) per hour and travel across an entire ocean!

Humans have explored only **about 5 percent** of the ocean depths.

About 20 million tons (18 million metric tons) of **gold is dissolved** in all of Earth's seawater!

Scientists calculate that it takes about **1,000 years** for a drop of water to circulate through all Earth's oceans.

Point Nemo,

a location in the southern Pacific Ocean, is the

most remote place on Earth.

It is more than 1,000 miles (1,600 kilometers) from land in any direction. At Point Nemo, you are closer to astronauts aboard the International Space Station than you are to anyone on Earth!

The world ocean would rise about 200 feet (60 meters) if the Greenland and Antarctic

ice sheets should suddenly melt.

New York City would be submerged, with only the tops of the tallest buildings above water.

A handful

of ocean water contains millions of

bacteria

and about one billion

viruses!

WORDS TO KNOW

artificial made by humans.

bioluminescent the ability of an animal to make its own light.

coast the land at the edge of an ocean or sea.

crust the outer surface of Earth.

current the movement of water in the open ocean.

erode to wear away.

evaporate to turn from a liquid into a gas.

food chain living things that are connected to each other because they depend on each other for food.

global warming a gradual increase in the overall temperature of Earth's atmosphere.

gravity the force that pulls objects together and makes objects fall to the ground on Earth.

nutrient something that plants and animals need to grow and be healthy.

plain a large area of flat land.

plankton very small ocean plants and animals.

ridge a long, raised area.

salt water water that contains salt. Salt water is found in seas and oceans.

sediment tiny pieces of sand and rock.

tectonic plate a section of Earth's crust.

tide the daily movement of water on and off the shore.

trench a long deep valley in the sea floor.

wave the movement of energy across the surface of the ocean.

QUIZ ANSWERS 1. English Channel; 2. South China Sea; 3. Atlantic Ocean; 4. Tasman Sea; 5. Arctic Ocean; 6. Indian Ocean; 7. Pacific Ocean; 8. Southern Ocean; 9. Mediterranean Sea; 10. Bering Sea; 11. Caribbean Sea; 12. Bay of Bengal; 13. Atlantic Ocean; 14. Indian Ocean; 15. Hudson Bay